For Such A Time As THIS

McDougal & Associates

Servants of Christ and Stewards of the Mysteries of God

For Such A Time As THIS

Making the Case for a Great Awakening and New Reformation of the Church

by

Lanny Swaim

Cover design by Cathy Sanders Design, Cicero, NY

Published by:

McDougal & Associates
18896 Greenwell Springs Road
Greenwell Springs, LA 70739
www.thepublishedword.com

McDougal & Associates is an organization dedicated to
spreading the Gospel of the Lord Jesus Christ to as many
people as possible in the shortest time possible.

ISBN: 978-1-940461-30-4
e-Book 978-1-940461-57-1

Printed in the U.S., the U.K. and Australia
For Worldwide Distribution

Dedication

I dedicate this book to **Miguel Escobar**, revivalist, author and longtime friend, who has ministered in over ninety nations, spreading revival fire with many signs, wonders and miracles following him wherever he goes. The day I met Miguel in the spring of 2000, the Lord told me I would travel with him for a period of time. That period of time started around two years later and lasted for several years. I traveled and ministered with him throughout the southeastern United States, from Northern Virginia to Orlando, Florida, spending much time around the Atlanta area and in North Carolina. We spent a week together with the Apache Indians in Arizona, three weeks in England and a week in Portugal.

While in England, we visited friends of Miguel's in Chichester. I later learned that some of my Quaker ancestors traveled from Chichester to Pennsylvania in the seventeenth century, becoming part of William Penn's *Holy Experiment*.

Acknowledgments

Thanks to Andy Sanders for connecting me with Steve Jones in Harrisburg, Pennsylvania, who set up my first ministry trip to Pennsylvania and has assisted with other trips.

Thanks to Darrell and Lorrie Fields for writing and publishing *The Seed of a Nation: Rediscovering America* and for their efforts to bring reconciliation between Native Americans and European Americans for the many injustices and blood shed following European settlers first coming to the New World. A very special thanks to Darrell and Lorrie for their encouragement and advice concerning the writing of this book.

To every thing there is a season, and a time to every purpose under the heaven.   Ecclesiastes 3:1

Surely the Lᴏʀᴅ Gᴏᴅ will do nothing, but he revealeth his secret unto his servants the prophets. The lion hath roared, who will not fear? The Lᴏʀᴅ Gᴏᴅ hath spoken, who can but prophesy?   Amos 3:7-8

Contents

Foreword by
Andy Sanders

As the Church sits, perched breath-lessly awaiting the arrival of the next Great Awakening, across the country and around the world believers search pro-phetic messages for understanding of the present season we are in on the timeline of history, seeking wisdom to navigate the transition into a new age of reformation. *For Such a Time As This: Making the Case for a Great Awakening and New Reformation of the Church*, by author Lanny Swaim, takes a fresh look at the possibility of such an awakening and reformation, dissecting the subject of salvation, focusing on the Great Commission as a reformation of nations.

Little did I realize, when I connected Lanny with Steve Jones of Harrisburg, Pennsylvania in 2016 (who then set up ministry engagements for Lanny in Pennsylvania and surrounding states) that it would lead to much more than an anointed apostle/prophetic teacher ministering in various church assemblies and home meetings. Lanny's meeting and connecting with Darrell and Lorrie Fields (authors of *The Seed of a Nation: Rediscovering America*) at a home meeting in Mechanicsburg and his discovery of his own Quaker ancestry going back to the time of William Penn and the founding of Pennsylvania set in motion spiritual revelation leading to the writing of this book.

Then, during Lanny's second ministry trip to Pennsylvania, in July of 2017, while he was attending a meeting in Lancaster where Chuck Pierce was ministering, Chuck prophesied of a spiritual connection between Pennsylvania and North Carolina, in reference to the coming awakening/revival.

As a native of North Carolina, Lanny delved deeper into the history of William

Penn's *Holy Experiment*, as Penn called Pennsylvania, and into the migration of his Quaker ancestors from Pennsylvania to North Carolina. His study led to the writing of this book, which explains the hardships our ancestors faced due to broken treaties and covenants initially made between the Native Americans and William Penn, treaties and covenants that were broken by those who did not share Penn's vision for a political model of the Kingdom of God in Pennsylvania.

Ultimately, Lanny's research led him to the conclusion that reconciliation must take place with those people groups wronged by our ancestors in order for this next Great Awakening to take place. While we are not responsible for the damage done historically to, not only the Native Americans, but also African Americans, we have been given the ministry of reconciliation (see 2 Corinthians 5:18-19).

Lanny's prophetic perspective, based on his research and spiritual revelation found in the pages of this book, will encourage, enlighten and excite you, as you discover our role individually as believers and corporately as the Church, in the next Great Awakening and Reformation of the Church.

Andy Sanders
International writer and speaker
www.capturingthesupernatural.com

Introduction

For quite some time now, well known and respected prophetic voices have been prophesying a great awakening coming to the United States. Some have even prophesied that it would begin with the passing of Billy Graham. I agree that Dr. Graham's passing was a pivotal moment, a line of demarcation on the timeline of history, signifying a major transition for the Church and the world.

Since the beginning of time, there have been certain moments that changed everything. I call them *kairos* moments.

In the Greek language, there are two words for *time*: (1) *chronos*, meaning chronological time, such as days on the calendar, and (2) *kairos*, meaning a specific moment in history, a moment pregnant with destiny.

One such moment occurred when God cut a covenant with Abram (meaning father), changing his name to Abraham (meaning father of many nations). That moment changed everything.

The birth of Jesus was another *kairos* moment, one that, again, changed everything. His birth was followed by His crucifixion, resurrection and ascension. These together brought radical change to God's plan for mankind and all of planet Earth. It was not that God's plan changed, but that the change was part of His plan.

Japan's bombing of Pearl Harbor on December 7, 1941, pulling the United States into World War II, signalled the end of the barbaric Japanese Empire. The war in the Pacific, in concert with the war in Europe, not only defeated and brought down the Imperialists of Japan, the Nazi's of Germany and the Fascists of Italy, but also established the United States as the world's great superpower and leader of the entire free world. That was truly a *kairos* moment.

Introduction

A more recent *kairos* moment occurred on September 11, 2001 (which has since become widely known simply as 9/11). What took place in the natural and spiritual realm that day signified and initiated a time of testing for the United States, the Church and the world. The tests and trials experienced by governments, societies, the Church corporately and individual believers since 9/11 are determining the future of the Church and the world.

But could it be that all of this is just the lead-up to another Great Awakening, a great revival that will sweep across America and the world? I believe it with all of my heart, and that will be the theme of the coming pages.

Lanny Swaim
Winnabow, North Carolina

Chapter 1

The Passing of Billy Graham and What It Means

Many are called, but few are chosen.
                                        Matthew 22:14

Billy Graham was definitely one of the chosen few. Like John the Baptist, Jeremiah and others, Billy's destiny seemed to be sealed before he exited his mother's womb. His simple message of personal salvation was probably the main catalyst that brought into existence a Christian mindset that transcended denominations, establishing an entire block of Christianity known as "Evangelicals." These evangelicals have not only been influential in the Church at large, but also in the American political arena.

We can safely conclude, therefore, that Billy Graham was a man born on the time-line of history to dominate an era that took Christianity beyond the advances the Protestant Reformation had begun, sparking what is to be the ultimate fulfillment of the Great Commission. As recorded in Mark 16:15, it says:

Go ye into all the world, and preach the gospel to every creature.

A Transition from One Era to Another

Jesus said:

*All power is given unto me in heaven and in earth. Go ye therefore, and **teach all nations**, baptizing them in the name of the Father, and of the Son, and of the Holy Ghost: teaching them to observe all the things whatsoever I have commanded you: and, lo, I am with you*

always, even unto the end of the world
[age].   Matthew 28:18-20
                        (emphasis added)

The Great Commission, as recorded in Mark 16:15 seems to emphasize the personal salvation message that Billy Graham preached. Perhaps Jesus was not only giving a command, but prophesying a future time when this evangelical aspect of the Great Commission would be restored to the Church. However, Matthew's account of the Great Commission seems to focus, not so much on *personal salvation*, but on the salvation of the nations.

While *personal salvation* is extremely important, it's really not the message that Jesus preached. Jesus preached the Gospel of the Kingdom, which focuses more on changing the world than on personal salvation. Actually, personal salvation is but the means to bring the Kingdom *"in earth as it is in Heaven"* (which Jesus taught us to pray), literally changing the nations of the world and, therefore, changing the world.

John, the disciple of Jesus, focused on this aspect of the Great Commission:

*For God so loved the **world** … .*

John 3:16 (Emphasis added)

Verily, verily, I say unto thee, Except a man be born again, he cannot see the kingdom of God.   Jesus in John 3:3

The Amplified Bible expands on the words *"see the kingdom"* to a much more specific *"he cannot ever see (know, be acquainted with, and experience) the kingdom of God."* This makes it clear to me that the primary purpose of being born again is not necessarily personal salvation, but to gain an understanding of and experience the Kingdom of God.

While the personal salvation message has as its main focus the concept of going to Heaven when the believer dies, the Gospel of the Kingdom focuses on bringing Heaven to Earth. This is, quite literally, a convergence of Heaven and Earth.

The fulfillment of this aspect of the Great Commission will change the world, bringing about the reality of Revelation 11:15:

The kingdoms [nations] *of this world are become the kingdoms* [Kingdom] *of our Lord, and of his Christ; and he shall reign for ever and ever.*

It has been revealed to me by the Spirit of God that the passing of Billy Graham prophetically signified a shift in the focus of the Great Commission, from the personal salvation message, to reaching entire nations with the Gospel, ultimately changing the political landscape of the whole world.

Chapter 2

The Beginning of a New Age

I am with you always, even unto the end of the world [age].

Jesus in Matthew 28:20

The Amplified Bible makes it clear that Jesus wasn't referring to the end of the *world* but, rather, the end of the *age*. I am convinced that a thorough study of prophetic scripture indicates that we are now transitioning from the Church Age into the Kingdom Age.

Billy Graham was a forerunner, and his life and ministry represented an era that opened the door to more than just another

24

era. Just as John the Baptist prepared the way for the first coming of Jesus, I believe that Billy Graham prepared the way for the coming of a new age, the Kingdom Age.

Jesus said He would be with us (believers) until the end of the *age*. Therefore I believe that, as we transition from the Church Age into the Kingdom Age, Jesus will not only be with us, but will become fully formed in us (see Galatians 4:19), enabling us to live a Kingdom lifestyle that will change the world. I also believe that, as many are prophesying, this changing of the world begins with the greatest spiritual awakening the Church and the world have ever known.

However, this spiritual awakening begins with a remnant. And, in my experience, the credentials of this remnant are the intense and severe tests and trials we have endured in recent years, and, in many cases, are still enduring.

God has always had a remnant. Sometimes it was one person or family, such as Noah, Abraham, Moses, etc. At other times, it was a people group. For instance, the Israelites were a remnant of all the nations on Earth. Then the Jews were a remnant of the people of Israel after they were scattered over the earth or annihilated. The first Christians were a remnant of those Jews.

During the Dark Ages, when the Roman Catholic Church persecuted true believers, there were numerous remnants that paid dearly for their faith, suffering horrendous torture and death.

In more recent times, there have been other remnants, trailblazers, on the cutting edge of where God is taking the Church and the world. Some of the better known have been the Quakers, the Moravians, the Methodists, the Anabaptists, the Pentecostals, the Charismatics, etc.

Today there is a new remnant. I believe this is the remnant Joel prophesied about:

And it shall come to pass, that whosoever shall call on the name of the LORD shall be delivered: for in mount Zion and in Jerusalem shall be deliverance, as the LORD

*hath said, and in the **remnant whom the** L<small>ORD</small> **shall call**.*
Joel 2:32 (emphasis added)

We know that originally the Old Testament prophecies were directed at Israel, but, I believe, most, if not all of them, had a dual application, and that second application was for the New Testament Church. Perhaps, in some cases, the New Testament application was even the stronger one.

Chapter 3

Hidden in the Secret Place

He that dwelleth in the secret place of the most High shall abide under the shadow of the Almighty. Psalm 91:1

This new remnant that I believe Joel prophesied about has been marked by the intense and severe tests and trials we have endured in recent years. However, for what seems to have been a very long time now and continuing to the present, we have been hidden from the world and from the Church, having been taken out of the greater Body of Christ. In some cases, we have remained covertly in the existing Church, separated from the world. This doesn't mean that we haven't been actively involved behind the scenes, interceding as we are being prepared, already making a major difference in the affairs of the Church and of the nations.

Our process of preparation has been one of coming to a much deeper trust in the Lord than we have ever known, finding that place of rest and peace that remains elusive to most of the Body of Christ. And, through this time of transition in our lives, our relationship with the Lord has become much more intimate, to the point that we not only positionally but experientially dwell in *the secret place of the Most High,"* hidden under His shadow.

But we won't remain hidden for long. Ours is not a walk that can remain hidden. As Jesus said:

> *For there is nothing covered, that shall not be revealed: and hid, that shall not be known.*   Matthew 10:26

Chapter 4

The Unveiling

For the earnest expectation of the creature waiteth for the manifestation [revelation/ unveiling] *of the sons of God.*

Romans 8:19

In the Hebrew culture of the Bible, the word *son* referred to a mature child, ready to receive his inheritance from his father, and to operate in all the authority of his father's name. So it is with this remnant that has been matured through a process of intense and severe tests and trials.

While we may not be one hundred percent there yet, we are closer than ever before, having tasted of the fulness of the Godhead indwelling us, enabling us to walk in greater authority than ever before, and having the assurance that we are in Christ and He is in us, that literally we are an extension of His hand and of His love.

Not only have we been prepared and positioned for the time at hand; we are about to and are even now being revealed, manifested or unveiled to the Church and the world. We are taking our rightful place of authority as ambassadors of the Kingdom of God.

Even though we face much opposition from the religious community and from the political and financial entities that think it is their destiny to rule the world, we cannot and will not be overcome. Rather, we will reign with the King of kings and Lord of lords, ultimately and literally bringing God's Kingdom *"in Earth as it is in Heaven."*

Chapter 5

The Revelation of Jesus Christ

The Revelation of Jesus Christ, which God gave unto him, to shew unto his servants things which must shortly come to pass; and he sent and signified it by his angel unto his servant John: who bare record of the word of God, and of the testimony of Jesus Christ, and of all things that he saw. Blessed is he that readeth, and they that hear the words of this prophecy, and keep those things which are written therein: for the time is at hand. Revelation 1:1-3

The book of Revelation is not a chronological order of the so-called end-times. Rather, it reveals Jesus as the King of kings and Lord of lords. Hence, it is synonymous with the manifestation of the sons of God. It is the unveiling of a people filled with all the fulness of the Godhead, taking their rightful place of authority and power on Earth, literally becoming an extension of God the Father, Son and Holy Spirit. As a result, they will pave the way for a convergence of Heaven and Earth, unlike anything known from the time of Creation until now.

Again, it all begins with a remnant. Since Adam and Eve were banished from the Garden of Eden, God has been in a process of restoration, reformation and transformation, with each new step toward those goals starting with a remnant.

The new remnant that is coming out of the Church today, whose purpose and destiny it is to be at the forefront of the greatest awakening the Church and the world has ever known, are none other than the manifested, revealed or unveiled sons of God (*sons* is not about gender and includes both men and women). They have been hidden for a season, but they are about to be made known.

The members of this covert remnant are not only laying the groundwork for a great awakening; they are pioneering the way for a total reformation of the Church, taking the Church far beyond the bounds of the Protestant Reformation of five hundred years ago.

But it doesn't stop there. They are paving the way for a total transformation of planet Earth, ultimately resulting in the nations of the world becoming the Kingdom of God (see Revelation 11:15). This will lead to the restoration of everything that was lost at the time of the fall of man in the Garden of Eden.

The tests and trials this remnant has endured were not intended to become a way of life, but, rather, the means to establish and enable them to walk in greater authority and power than ever before, fulfilling their destiny to ultimately bring Heaven to Earth.

Chapter 6

It All Begins with a Seed

*Except a corn of wheat fall into the ground
and die, it abideth alone: but if it die, it
bringeth forth much fruit.*
                              Jesus in John 12:24

In John 12:24 we see a spiritual principal that has been in play from Creation until the present.

In Genesis 1:26, God said, *"Let us make man in our image, after our likeness."* Then Genesis 1:27 says, *"So God created man in his own image, in the image of God created he him; male and female created He them."* What happened to *likeness*? There is no more mention of *likeness* in verse 27.

The Hebrew word for *image* is *tselm*, which means "a representative figure or a representative of." The Hebrew word for *likeness* is *dmuwth*, which, based on several definitions, has to do with character.

One day, while reading Genesis 1:27, I realized that Adam was made in God's image, to be His representative on Earth, but he was not created in God's likeness (again, there is no more mention of likeness in verse 27). When I first saw this, I exclaimed, "God, You created man in Your image, but You didn't create him in Your likeness. And this was right after You said, *'Let us make man in our image after our likeness.'* So, what's the deal?"

Immediately I realized that image can be created. Advertising agencies do it all the time. But character cannot be created. Character has to be developed.

Adam and Eve had to fall, first becoming like God in their knowledge of good and evil (see Genesis 3:22), in order for Jesus, *"the last Adam"* (see 1 Corinthians 15:45), to come and make it possible for mankind to begin to possess the character of God, which is unadulterated, pure and genuine love.

In essence, man was created sinless but not perfect. In order to be perfected, sin, with all its consequences, had to enter the picture. It is only in overcoming sin and the flesh (self) that we become like God in character.

This was all part of God's plan. He created Adam and Eve, knowing they would fall. And, I might add, knowing they *had to* fall. There was no other way for God to have a man like Himself, possessing His character.

So, the tranquility of the Garden of Eden and the immortal physical body that Adam was created with had to die, becoming a seed, which would one day produce the last Adam, Jesus, who would learn obedience by the things He suffered (see Hebrews 5:8).

While Jesus lived a sinless life, his physical body was mortal, like Adam's became because of sin. It wasn't until Jesus was resurrected that His physical body became immortal. However, it still wasn't perfected. He walked out of that tomb with the scars of the crucifixion still in His hands, feet and side. So, when will His body be perfected? In the third day of the Church.

Chapter 7

The Significance of the Third Day

Behold, I cast out devils, and I do cures to day and to morrow, and **the third day I shall be perfected**.

Jesus in Luke 13:32
(emphasis added)

Beloved, be not ignorant of this one thing, that one day is with the Lord as a thousand years and a thousand years as one day.

2 Peter 3:8

Jesus walked out of the tomb on the third day after the crucifixion, but His body was not perfected while He was in the tomb.

His resurrection made His physical body immortal, but He still had the scars of the crucifixion in His hands, feet and side. I ask again: When will His body be perfected? **In the third day (millennium) of the Church.**

Peter spoke of many things in the two books of the Bible that bear his name, but he put great emphasis on this one thing (telling his readers not to be ignorant of it): that a day is with the Lord as a thousand years and a thousand years as a day. Personally, I believe that this mathematical comparison is a key to understanding the entire Bible.

The Bible focuses on seven thousand years of history, and a thorough study of Daniel's seventy weeks indicates that God has made provision for the Hebrew calendars and the Gregorian calendar. The prophecies of Daniel only work when understood utilizing the general Hebrew calendar (twelve months of thirty days each) and the Gregorian calendar.

So, with that in mind, we are now entering the seventh day (millennium) since Creation, according to the Gregorian calendar, and the third day (millennium) of the Church. And I must add: what a remnant of believers is experiencing today is confirmation that this is where we are on the timeline of history.

There is another Old Testament prophecy that I believe is specifically about this remnant:

Come, and let us return unto the LORD: for he hath torn, and he will heal us; he hath smitten, and he will bind us up. After **two days** *will he revive us: in* **the third day** *he will raise us up, and we shall live in his sight.* Hosea 6:1-2 (emphasis added)

After 9/11, like other believers I know, I experienced a time of severe and intense tests and trials in my life. I was blindsided by the reality that nothing was working for me as it had in previous years.

I had a successful business, a very good marriage and a relatively comfortable existence. But then, quite suddenly, I couldn't seem to make enough money to pay all the bills. While I had a good reputation as a paint contractor, with much repeat business and rarely having to compete with anyone else for the jobs I got, I now just couldn't seem to earn enough. Something was always happening to steal my profit and my operating finances.

At first, I started borrowing a little here and a little there for payroll and operating expenses, thinking I would replace it when I got paid for the next job. But the money never got put back, and in a two-year period, I found myself in $70,000 worth of business debt that I saw no way of ever repaying.

As you can imagine, this business debt began to affect my personal finances, which eventually put a strain on my marriage.

I did everything I knew to do. I prayed, utilizing all the faith I thought I knew how to operate in. I confessed the promises found in the Bible. And I rebuked the devil—a lot. Nothing seemed to work.

At perhaps my lowest point, I told the Lord, "You can have it all: my business, my house, my wife and my dog." Then I added, "I know Your voice, and I'm going to continue to obey You, even if it costs me everything." It nearly did, and I know others who experienced similar tests and trials in their lives and did lose everything.

Then early one Monday morning in 2003, while lying on my couch unable to sleep, I was praying in the Spirit and heard the Lord say, "Put the ball back in My court."

It was the first time He had ever spoken to me in a cliché.

I said, "Lord, I didn't know I was carrying the ball, but I put it back in Your court. I'm not doing another thing until You do something."

At 7:00 that morning my wife came to me with a word she had received from the Lord at the same time I was hearing from Him lying there on the couch. Her revelation began a series of events that ultimately turned my situation around and made provision to pay off the business debt I had accumulated.

But the tests and trials didn't end immediately. In fact, they continued for two more years. Then, God sat me down for eight years after that, not allowing me to do any ministry except writing, sending out emails (which would eventually become books.)

During that eight-year period (eight being the number for new beginnings in the Scriptures), I did much reflecting on the purpose of the four years of tests and trials (the biblical meaning of the number four having to do with God setting things in order, relating specifically to destiny. The four sides of a square are equal and symbolize strength).

Through all of this, I came to realize that God was trying to do a work in me that could not be accomplished without me experiencing the intense tests and trials I had been going through. While I had been rebuking the devil, I was really rebuking God. He was the One orchestrating my life in such a way that nothing was working, in an effort to bring me to the end of myself.

I came to realize that I didn't trust God nearly as much as I thought I did. My trust was based on circumstances. And circumstances are not the determination of whether or not the Word of God is working in our lives. The greatest faith is to believe God's Word, even when it appears not to be working. I am convinced, that until we can say with Job, *"Though he slay me, yet will I trust in him"* (Job 13:15), that we *don't* really trust Him. We just *think* we do.

With my newfound trust came a rest and peace that I had not known before, and that, I believe, is currently elusive to most of the members of the Body of Christ. The writer of Hebrews spoke of a rest that remains for the people of God (see Hebrews 4:9). I believe this is a prophetic scripture that could not be realized until this day, the seventh millennium since Creation.

What is the significance of the seventh day in the Scriptures? It is the Sabbath, and this current millennium is the Sabbath of all Sabbaths. It is the Sabbath that all the Sabbaths of the Law and the seventh day of Creation, point the way to. It is *"that day"* and *"the day of the Lord,"* spoken of so much throughout the Bible.

Not until this day could a people begin to fully realize *"the rest that remaineth."* And like everything God has done in history, it has begun with a remnant.

A by-product of this rest, which a greater trust is producing in the people of this remnant, is the "*peace ... which passeth all understanding*":

> *Be careful for nothing; but in every thing by prayer and supplication with thanksgiving let your requests be made known unto God. And the peace of God, which passeth all understanding, shall keep your hearts and minds through Christ Jesus.*
> Philippians 4:6-7

To *"be careful for nothing"* means that we don't care. Peter told us to cast all our care on the Lord, who cares for us (see 1 Peter 5:7).

In our society today, the word *care* is used synonymously with the word *love*. But care is not love. The definition of *care* is, among other things, "worry, anxiety, mental anguish, etc." Care produces strife, and strife is a killer.

To be free of care is to find that *"rest that remaineth"* and the *"peace that passeth all understanding,"* which keeps our hearts and minds. This is how our minds are renewed to the Word of God (see Romans 12:2).

This is also how we become like God, possessing His character. It is the process that produces in us a dying to self, literally becoming emptied of self, making room for God the Father, Son and Holy Spirit to fully indwell us (see Galatians 4:19, AMPC and Colossians 2:9-10), ultimately living His life in and through us.

This removes from us all pressure to perform. We no longer have to strive to become like Christ. He has made provision for us to become like Him. That reality, that truth, is the destiny of the third-day Church. It is a process that has begun with a remnant, and will ultimately bring the entire Church to the fulfillment of Ephesians 5:27, becoming a glorious Church, without spot, wrinkle or any such thing, holy and without blemish.

In a word, this Church will be *perfect*. Yes, it is in this third day of the Church that

Jesus, the Head, will be perfected in Jesus, the Body of Christ, literally becoming one and the same.

It is this perfecting process that is preparing and positioning a people to be at the forefront of the greatest spiritual awakening the Church, the United States and the rest of the world has ever known.

Chapter 8

Centuries in the Making

Whom shall he teach knowledge? And whom shall he make to understand doctrine? Them that are weaned from the milk, and drawn from the breasts. For precept must be upon precept, precept upon precept; line upon line, line upon line; here a little, and there a little.

Isaiah 28:9-10

Ultimately, the process of dying to self, which is producing in God's remnant a maturity beyond what only a few have experienced in the past, is possible only because of the numerous *kairos* moments in history that have brought us to where we are

today. God's plan of redemption, reconciliation, restitution and transformation—which
is the Gospel of the Kingdom—would have
no future without the past.

Just as it took the fall of the first Adam to
make way for the last Adam, it has taken all
the events of history to bring us to where
we are today.

I emphasize again: this is uniquely the
seventh day since Creation and the third
day of the Church, which is, undoubtedly,
"the Day of the Lord!"

With that in mind, I would like to look
at a specific seed that was planted more
than three hundred years ago on the North
American continent, a seed that was actually
conceived in England and then planted in
what is now the Commonwealth of Pennsylvania, in our modern-day U.S.A.

Chapter 9

"The Seed of a Nation"

My God that has given it [Pennsylvania]
me through many difficulties, will, I be-
lieve, bless and make it the seed of a nation.
Written by William Penn on March 6, 1681

William Penn had a vision for establishing a model of the Kingdom of God in Earth as in Heaven, and he called Pennsylvania "a Holy Experiment." The man was way ahead of his time, and yet, he was right on time.

It should be pointed out that William Penn's vision was one of freedom and not coercion. He realized that government best served the people when godly men were in leadership positions and that godly principals were the best foundation for just laws. Still, he was an advocate for the separation of Church and State, having been imprisoned several times in England because of a state-controlled church.

William Penn's Holy Experiment was not one of a Christian nation, but, rather, one that ensured the free exercise of religion. To conflate William Penn's work with a mandate to make America a Christian nation is in no way my intention for this writing. To measure the progress of the Gospel by its progress within the nation state was the mistake made in the fourth century when the Emperor Constantine made it legal to be a Christian in the Roman Empire, and then Emperor Theodosius made it a law that all Roman citizens *had to be* Christians.

However, I do want to point out that the current political climate of the United States is moving us into a position that is allowing and paving the way for a great spiritual awakening among the people of the nation, and a new reformation of the Church, ultimately playing a role in God's unfolding plan for a total transformation of planet Earth and the restitution of all things.

The following is a brief history of William Penn's life and the founding of Pennsylvania:

• In May of 1661, under King Charles II, the English Parliament passed laws known as the Clarendon Code, restricting the free exercise of religion.

• That next year, in May of 1662, Parliament passed the Quaker Act, making it illegal for Quakers to assemble for worship in groups larger than five. (The Quakers [Society of Friends] had been founded by George Fox in 1647.)

• William Penn, born in 1644, attended Oxford but was expelled after two years for being too religious and a nonconformist, due to the Quaker influence on his young life.

• Quakers believed that the Scriptures were to be obeyed, that God spoke to them and that they were to be in constant communion with divine authority.

- King Charles II, as head of the Church of England, considered the Quakers to be a threat to the State.

- William Penn became a Quaker in 1667 at the age of twenty-two.

- William Penn's father was an admiral in the English Navy. Admiral William Penn had been knighted by the king in 1660. He was a very wealthy man who loaned money to the crown.

- Young William Penn, the Quaker, was an embarrassment to his father, Sir William Penn, and was arrested several times while in his twenties because of his religious beliefs.

- Had young Penn's father not have been Sir William Penn, he might have met the fate of many Quakers and died in prison. Instead, he was released numerous times.

- Sir William Penn died in 1670 at the age of forty-nine. Before his death, he had young William removed from prison and called to his side. He exhorted his son to follow his conscience and gave him his entire estate.

- After his father's death, young William petitioned the crown for land in the New World.
- King Charles II, in an effort to settle the debt he owed the Penns and also to rid England of the Quakers, granted young William Penn 28,000,000 acres in the New World.
- In this way, at the age of thirty-six, William Penn became the largest private land owner in the world.
- On March 6, 1681, William Penn wrote, "My God that has given it [Pennsylvania] me through many difficulties, will, I believe bless and make it *the seed of a nation.*"

Even though vast lands in what is now Pennsylvania had been granted to William Penn by the king, the young Penn signed treaties with and made covenants with the inhabitants of the land, settling only in areas agreed upon with the Native Americans, enabling the English settlers to remain at peace with their native counterparts during his lifetime and for several years thereafter.

Our founding fathers drafted the U.S. Constitution modeled after William Penn's Constitution for Pennsylvania. He wrote his constitution, reasoning that without God his government would not succeed. However, he also believed that government should not force or restrict religion, but that all people should be free to worship and obey God as they saw fit.

After William Penn's death, his ideals were eventually abandoned, and the Native Americans living in Pennsylvania were badly mistreated, and treaties and covenants were broken. However, the seed had been planted and has remained until today, having some effect, but being primarily dormant.

One of my ancestors, John Allen, came to Pennsylvania with William Penn. His son, John Allen II, traveled to North Carolina and there purchased acreage at Snow Camp. Unfortunately, John Allen II died before he could move his family to North Carolina. Later, his widow did move the family there and then remarried. One of her descendants, Nereus Barker, a Quaker preacher, was my great-grandfather. Nereus was also a descendant of Samuel Barker, who bought land from William Penn in what later became Delaware.

On my ministry trip to Pennsylvania in July, 2017, I attended a meeting where Chuck Pierce was speaking. He prophesied of a spiritual connection between Pennsylvania and North Carolina.

During my ministry trip to Pennsylvania in May of 2018, I met Darrell and Lorrie Fields, authors of the book, *The Seed of a Nation: Rediscovering America*. [1] Most of the facts compiled about William Penn and the founding of Pennsylvania in this writing were taken from that book.

---

1. Scotland, PA, Healing the Land Publishing: 2008

Chapter 10

A Revival Prophesied for Many Years

I have found favor with you here in Eastern North Carolina. I will personally visit you. There will be a revival greater than that of the great Wales Revival at the turn of the century [the 20th Century]. *There will be kings and leaders who will come from north and south and east and west to study the Eastern North Carolina phenomenon.*

A prophetic word delivered by Derek Prince, Sunday, April 6, 1975 at Deliverance Evangelistic Temple in Jacksonville, NC

As Derek Prince finished giving this prophecy that April morning in 1975, someone in the middle of the congregation stood up, holding his Bible in his hand and yelling, "I've got something. I've got something!" Loudly he began to read Zephaniah 2:6:

And the sea coast shall be dwellings and cottages for shepherds, and folds for flocks.

Four months later, in August of 1975, the Onslow County Full Gospel Business Men's Fellowship was holding a dinner meeting at King's Restaurant on Gum Branch Road, between Jacksonville and Richlands, NC. Charles Woodhouse, a medical doctor, was the guest speaker that night.

After Dr. Woodhouse was introduced, he said, "I don't know how to tell you this, but I don't have a thing to tell you tonight. I have been wrestling with the Lord for the last two weeks, asking Him to give me what He wanted me to tell you, and He hasn't given me a thing.

"This afternoon, as I was praying in my bedroom, at the guesthouse where I am staying, I got angry with God for not giving me anything to say. I told Him I was going to open my Bible and tell you whatever I opened to. As I opened my Bible, it opened to Zephaniah.

"I said, 'Zephaniah? Who is he? What did he ever do?'

"I read through the first chapter and didn't see anything. I started on the second chapter, and there it was in verse 6:

And the sea coast shall be dwellings and cottages for shepherds, and folds for flocks.

"Today, as I flew in over Emerald Isle, on my way to land, I somehow felt that the Lord has found favor with you here in Eastern North Carolina, that He is going to visit you."

The scripture that was read after Derek Prince gave his word on April 6, 1975 was the same one being read at the FGBMFI meeting in August of that year. I believe it was the complete word that God wanted to bring forth, and it seems clear to me that

Zephaniah 2:6 is referring to house meetings/house churches.

When I met Darrell and Lorrie Fields, I shared with them a vision I had been given by the Lord, for networks of house churches, connected by apostolic training centers. Darrell commented that the implementation of this vision would sustain the next great awakening.

All the awakenings, revivals or moves of God in the past have come and gone. But I believe that the awakening we are now entering into will perpetually continue until the Kingdom of God is established, not only in individuals, but in the political arenas and nations of the world, bringing about the fulfillment of Revelation 11:15:

> *The kingdoms* [nations] *of this world are become the kingdoms* [Kingdom] *of our Lord, and of his Christ; and he shall reign for ever and ever.*

As I was reading Darrell's book, *The Seed of a Nation*, the first time, the Lord very clearly spoke to me and said, "The revival that Derek Prince prophesied about Eastern North Carolina has to begin in Pennsylvania, because Pennsylvania is 'the seed of the nation.' "

Many Quakers migrated from Pennsylvania to North Carolina, so there is a spiritual connection between these two states, as Chuck Pierce prophesied in Lancaster, Pennsylvania in July of 2017. As I have already stated, I have Quaker ancestry on my mother's side of the family going back to John Allen and Samuel Barker. On my father's side, my grandmother was a Wright before marrying Virgil Swaim. The Wrights were also Quakers. So I have a rich spiritual heritage on both sides of the family.

When Andy Sanders of 5 Fold Media in Cicero, New York first put me in contact with Steve Jones in Harrisburg, Pennsylvania and Steve then set up my first ministry trip to Pennsylvania, I had no idea where this newfound connection with Pennsylvania would take me.

At the time, I was somewhat aware of my Quaker ancestry, but I had no idea that my ancestors first came to Pennsylvania from England, and that they were a part of William Penn's Holy Experiment.

I have been something of a keeper of the Derek Prince prophecy for Eastern North Carolina, but I was unaware that the fulfillment of it depended on the sprouting of the dormant seed that is Pennsylvania.

Shortly after leaving Baltimore, Maryland, headed toward York, Pennsylvania, on my ministry trip there in May of 2018, I sensed that I was driving onto holy ground. A couple in Waynesboro, Pennsylvania who had become good friends, told me they had a similar experience on a recent trip when they crossed the border of North Carolina.

Interestingly, when Derek Prince gave his prophetic word in Jacksonville, North Carolina all those many years ago, the same word, almost word-for-word, was given on the same day in the Tidewater area of Virginia. The only difference was that the

Tidewater word said that the revival was coming out of the Tidewater area.

Perhaps the fulfillment of these prophetic words about revival and the fruit of the seed planted by William Penn will happen so suddenly that it will appear to come about simultaneously throughout this great nation that I believe God founded to be a beacon of His light and freedom to the entire world.

Again, I must emphasize, that like any harvest, it has to begin with a seed. And Pennsylvania is the seed of this nation.

Chapter 11

The Conditions to Be Met

… visiting the iniquity of the fathers upon the children, and upon the children's children, unto the third and to the fourth generation. Exodus 34:7
(spoken to Moses by the Lord God)

After the death of William Penn, his three sons became the proprietors of Pennsylvania. They were not always in agreement about the governing of Pennsylvania, and perhaps didn't share their father's passion for establishing a model of the Kingdom of God in the New World. Eventually, treaties and covenants with the Indians were broken and, as a result, much blood was shed, staining the soil of William Penn's Holy Experiment.

With the French venturing into the Ohio Valley and western Pennsylvania from Canada and new English settlers who didn't share the Quaker beliefs settling into Pennsylvania and the surrounding colonies, William Penn's vision dimmed ... until it was all but forgotten.

Eventually, the Moravians moved into the area and made an effort to make peace with the Indians, converting some of them to Christ. Their influence, however, could not combat the greed and immorality of many of the English and French settlers. Ultimately, all of this led to the French and Indian War, with both sides attempting to rally the Indians against the other side.

The various tribes and nations of Native Americans, even though most were never converted to Christianity, believed in a Great Spirit that created us all. They were people of integrity, whose bond was their word. They had no comprehension of a people who had no regard or respect for covenants and treaties. After years of broken covenants and treaties at the hands of the "Christian" settlers, eventually the Indians felt they had no choice but to fight for what was rightfully theirs. Apparently the fact that they were a trusting people, who resorted to violence only as a last resort, led to their conquest and demise.

When I met Darrell Fields in Mechanicsburg, PA, he told of recently visiting the Lenape (also called Delaware) Indians in Oklahoma, where they eventually settled, along with the Cherokees who were driven out of North Carolina. The Lenape were the first Native Americans William Penn met when he first came to Pennsylvania. Darrell said the Lenape still speak of William Penn with high regard, giving him great honor.

William Penn planted a righteous seed, but the sins of those who came after him stained the ground of his Holy Experiment with much blood, shed by both the Native Americans and the white settlers.

The fourth chapter of Genesis gives an account of the first murder, when Cain killed

his brother Abel. In verse ten, God told
Cain that the voice of his brother's blood
was crying out to Him from the ground.
The blood that was spilled and the damage
done mercilessly to the Native Americans is
crying out to God, just as Abel's blood did
all those years ago.

Perhaps racial tensions between blacks
and whites in the United States are not
only the result of great injustices committed against African Americans, but are also
the result of the great injustices against the
Native Americans. While we are not guilty
of the sins of our ancestors, our present
generations are still feeling the effects of the
terrible injustices our ancestors committed.

We are told, in 2 Corinthians 5:18-19, that
we (believers in Christ) have been given *"the
ministry of reconciliation"* and that God has committed to us *"the word of reconciliation"* (which
is the Gospel of the Kingdom). So, even though
I am not guilty of the sins my ancestors committed, I can bring reconciliation for those sins.

If we are to see the great awakening that is
being prophesied, I believe we must first re-

The Conditions to Be Met

pent for the sins of our ancestors, by taking action to reconcile with Native Americans and African Americans, who suffered many injustices at the hands of the white settlers from Europe. Perhaps this is the primary thing holding back revival in our land.

Chapter 12

For Such a Time as This

… who knoweth whether thou art come to
the kingdom for such a time as this?

Esther 4:14

Before the fall of man in the Garden of
Eden, God had a plan that would eventually
perfect His creation. All the sins committed, all the evil done, all the suffering and
death of the past six thousand years has not
changed God's plan one bit. Today God is
calling out of religion and out of the world
system a remnant of mankind, to initiate
restitution and reconciliation for all those
harmed and victimized by whomever for
whatever reason, ultimately pioneering

the way for the Kingdom of Heaven, also known as the Kingdom of God, to fully manifest in Earth as in Heaven.

Those of the remnant are trailblazers, cutting a trail for many more to follow. They have been marked by the severe and intense tests and trials they have endured and are emerging overcomers, walking in greater authority and power than any previous generation.

The recent tests and trials they have been subjected to have produced in them a dying to self unlike anything they have experienced before. Being emptied of self, they can now be fully indwelled by the fulness of the Godhead (see Colossians 2:8-10).

While I believe that all of us in this remnant are still in the process of this emptying of self and becoming fully indwelled by all of God there is, we have tasted of it and are perhaps closer to it than any other generation from the past.

But we don't have to wait until we are one hundred percent there to make a difference. Even now we can take great strides toward the convergence of Heaven and Earth that is the destiny of all of creation.

Like Jesus, our Example, we must be about our Father's business (see Luke 2:49). Like Jesus, we will do the things He did and even greater things (see John 14:12), because…

Surely we were born for such a time as this!

Chapter 13

A Glorious Future

*And there shall be upon every high moun-
tain, and upon every high hill, rivers and
streams of waters in* **the day of the great
slaughter, when the towers fall***. More-
over the light of the moon shall be as the
light of the sun, and the light of the sun
shall be sevenfold, as the light of seven
days, in the day that the* Lord *bindeth up
the breach of his people, and healeth the
stroke of their wound.* Isaiah 30:25-26
(emphasis added)

When those twin towers fell in New York
City on 9/11, the significance of it was more
than the time of intense and severe testing

and trials that ensued. That day catapulted the United States of America toward once again becoming the world's great super-power and a beacon of freedom for the entire world.

Interestingly, 9/11 occurred right after we had crossed the threshold of a new day (the new millennium), the seventh day since Creation and the third day of the Church, with the possibilities of this new day being limitless. As we move into the beginning stages of the greatest spiritual awakening the Church, the United States and the world has ever known, at first it may appear that everything is getting darker instead of brighter. But we must remember, according to the Genesis account of Creation and the Hebrew calendars, that each new day begins at evening. So, the beginning of the day leads into the darkest part of the day, before the dawn brings new light.

Isaiah declared:

Arise, shine; for thy light is come, and the glory of the LORD is risen upon thee. For,

A Glorious Future

behold, the darkness shall cover the earth, and gross darkness the people: but the L<small>ORD</small> *shall arise upon thee, and his glory shall be seen upon thee. And the Gentiles* [nations] *shall come to thy light, and kings to the brightness of thy rising.*

Isaiah 60:1-5

This, the greatest of all spiritual awakenings, will produce a new reformation of the Church, and will ultimately bring about a total transformation of planet Earth. Then the nations of this world will become the Kingdom of God, enabling the restitution of all things.

Never has there been a day like this day. Never has there been a time like this time. And I must say it again …

Surely we were born For Such a Time As This!

Afterword

I believe we should continually be seeking avenues to bring reconciliation between Native Americans, African Americans and European Americans. As I have endeavored to do this, the Lord gave me a prophetic word specifically for African Americans. I asked two friends— Alveda King, daughter of A.D. King and niece of Dr. Martin Luther King, Jr. and Pauline Hankins, an African-American district court judge in North Carolina—to critique it for me, which they graciously did. Because I am of European descent, I felt I should get their viewpoint before publishing it.

As a white, European American, I consider it a great honor to have been given this word to pass on to my black brothers and sisters, in hope of bringing reconciliation between our races, especially within the Body of Christ.

A Prophetic Word for African-American Christians

Who hath heard such a thing? Who hath seen such things? Shall the earth be made to bring forth in one day? Or shall a nation be born at once? For as soon as Zion travailed, she brought forth her children.
                                        Isaiah 66:8

We all know the story of Joseph. He was sold into slavery by his own brothers and separated from his father and family at the tender age of seventeen. Then, in Egypt, he was unjustly accused and thrown into prison. But through all of this (his trials lasted for thirteen years), God was with Joseph, maturing him while preparing and positioning him to become the number two man to the most powerful king on earth at the time.

That promotion came suddenly. In one day, Joseph went from being a prisoner who had been a slave to being a powerful ruler in the great empire of Egypt.

Because of the position God placed Joseph in, he was able to save Egypt and the entire region from famine. This included his father and the very brothers who had sold him into slavery. As a result, his father and brothers came to live with him in Egypt, prospering in their temporary home … that is, until a very different Pharaoh came to power and became fearful of the Hebrew people, considering them to be a powerful threat to Egypt.

We all know the story of how the Israelite people became slaves in Egypt, living there for more than four hundred years. It appeared that history was repeating itself. First, Joseph had been a slave, and now his descendants were all slaves. But just as God had positioned Joseph for greatness, He was also positioning Joseph's descendants for greatness.

We also know the story of how God raised up Moses to deliver his people from

Pharaoh, at great expense to Pharaoh and the Egyptians. The Israelites had travailed in Egypt as slaves for so many years, but then in one night, they formed a great and wealthy nation, and Moses led them forth into the wilderness and eventually to the Promised Land.

This wasn't the last time God plundered the Egyptians to save His chosen people. When the tiny nation of Israel won the Six Day War against a much larger, opposing military machine in 1967, the Egyptians were sent fleeing for home across the desert, minus all of their weapons. God had done it again.

A Recent Historic and Modern-Day Parallel

Now all these things happened unto them for ensamples: and are written for our admonition. 1 Corinthians 10:11

Now, in the remaining pages of this book, I want to speak prophetically to you about another group of people. There is a definite parallel between the Israelites of old and the African Americans who were brought here as slaves. Just like Joseph and his descendants, Africans were brought to America against their will and forced into slavery, travailing for many years under the cruelty of oppression by white slave owners. Like the Israelites, their travail was not to be in vain.

When President Abraham Lincoln freed the slaves and the Union won the American Civil War, it appeared that the travail of so many African slaves had given birth to freedom for their race in America. The truth was that their freedom was very limited, especially in the South, where they continued to face racial injustice and inequality for many more years.

Then God raised up a generation led by Martin Luther King, Jr. and others, men and women willing to defy the so-called white supremacy by taking a peaceful stand against intimidating violence. Eventually laws were changed, and greater strides were taken to ensure the equality and opportunity that Abraham Lincoln and Martin Luther King, Jr. had envisioned.

Still, the battle for freedom was not over. The same Federal Government that had done away with slavery and passed laws to ensure equal opportunity for blacks in an integrated society, once again enslaved many in poverty with their seemingly-compassionate welfare and government assistance programs.

But that, perhaps, was not the worst enemy African Americans have had to face in modern-day America. Actual genocide has taken place in the United States under the guise of a woman's right to choose. While abortion has affected all races in America, it has especially targeted the African-American community and, as a result, millions of the unborn have been denied the right to life, liberty and the pursuit of happiness that the United States Declaration of Independence speaks of. Is it any wonder that some African Americans seem to have given up hope of ever being truly free?

Recently I heard the Lord say, "Just as I positioned the Israelites in Egypt, I have positioned Africans in the United States." The white man saw slavery as a means to prosper, Africans saw slavery as an injustice, but God saw it as a means to position people for greatness.

Positioned for Greatness

Thou shalt increase my greatness, and comfort me on every side. Psalm 71:21

I believe that the African-American Christian community in the United States will be at the forefront of the next great spiritual awakening in this nation. And it won't be the first time they have been at the forefront of a great revival movement here.

In 1906, revival broke out at a house on Bonnie Brae Street in Los Angles, California. The people who worshiped there were led by an African-American pastor, William Seymour of Louisiana.

As the crowd quickly outgrew the house on Bonnie Brae Street, Pastor Seymour moved the revival to a renovated stable on Azusa Street. There what has become known as The Azusa Street Revival was born. Modern-day Pentecostal churches still consider their beginning to be that Azusa Street Revival, which was made up of a mix of black and white Americans.

Saints, God has made it clear to me that once again He will position African Americans at the forefront of the great move of God that is about to take place in the United States. While this move will include many other nations, and has, in fact, already begun in other nations, it will propel the United States into a spiritual rebirth that will make this nation, founded on Judeo-Christian principals, once again a great and powerful force to be reckoned with on the world stage.

I must add (and I say this prophetically), we will stand with Israel as never before, our two nations becoming the spiritual and political leaders of the world. We are already seeing this happen under the leadership of the Trump Administration.

I am a white man who was born in the segregated southern United States. I grew up in a world that was full of prejudice and hatred. But as a teenager in the 1960s, even before I was born again, I began to see how wrong that was. Since being born again and as God has developed His character in me, I have come to love and respect all races.

While I am not guilty of the sins of my ancestors, I do feel a responsibility to bring healing wherever and whenever I can. Perhaps that is why God has given me this prophetic word for the Christian, African-American community in the United States.

In addition to the word I have already shared in this article, I hear the Lord saying this:

You [African-American Christians] are about to experience greatness in a measure you have never before realized. Surely you were born *For Such a Time As This!*

Surely we were all born *For Such a Time As This!*

Afterword

To my African-American brothers and sisters, I say (not prophetically, but out of the character of God that dwells within me), I love you and appreciate you for who you are, and I look forward with great anticipation to who we are becoming.

The Lord is growing to fulness in His Body, where there is neither male nor female, Jew nor Gentile, black nor white, etc. (see Galatians 3:28-29). We are all one in Christ, Abraham's seed, and heirs according to the promise.

So be it!

In Summary

And they that shall be of thee shall build the old waste places: thou shalt raise up the foundations of many generations; and thou shalt be called, The repairer of the breach, The restorer of paths to dwell in.
Isaiah 58:12

And all things are of God, who hath reconciled us to himself by Jesus Christ, and hath given to us the ministry of reconciliation: ... and hath committed unto us the word of reconciliation.   2 Corinthians 5:18-19

Blessed are the peacemakers … .
Matthew 5:9

All the revivals (awakenings, moves of God, outpourings of the Spirit, etc.) of the past were necessary and useful, but were not, in and of themselves, complete; nor did they finalize, in any way, God's plan and purpose for mankind. This next Great Awakening, which will produce a new Reformation of the Church, will be the beginning of the ending that Jesus referred to as Himself four times in the book of Revelation:

I am the Alpha and Omega, the beginning and the ending, saith the Lord, which is, and which was, and which is to come, the Almighty. Revelation 1:8

I am the Alpha and Omega, the first and the last … . Revelation 1:11

And he that sat upon the throne said, Behold, I make all things new. And he said unto me, Write: for these words are true and faithful. And he said unto me, It is done. I am Alpha and Omega, the beginning and the end. I will give unto him that is athirst of the fountain of the water of life freely. He that overcometh shall inherit all things; and I will be his God, and he shall be my son. Revelation 21:5-7

I am Alpha and Omega, the beginning and the end, the first and the last.
Revelation 22:13

As I was waking up one morning recently, I very clearly heard the Lord say, "I am the Alpha and the Peep." Immediately I realized that He was trying to reveal something to me, which I quickly understood to be more of a confirmation than a new revelation.

To peep means "to look quickly and secretively at something, especially through a narrow opening." There are those in the Body of Christ today who are a remnant at the most and perhaps even a remnant within a remnant, who are getting a glimpse, a peep, into the Ending, the Omega that Jesus described Himself as four times in the book of Revelation.

The number four, in scripture, is representative of setting things in order, especially

In Summary

in relation to destiny. There are four seasons, four corners of the Earth or directions (north, south, east and west), four Gospel accounts in the Bible, and a square has four corners and four sides, with each side being equal, signifying strength. A four-cornered object made with forty-five-degree angles is strong and secure. So the fact that Jesus said four times in Revelation that He is the beginning and the ending is establishing a truth that sets things in order.

We tend to think of this *beginning* and *ending* as having to do with a timeline, but that viewpoint gives us a very limited understanding of what Jesus is trying to communicate here. He, Jesus the Person, the Spirit that is God, is the Beginning and the Ending, which not only encompasses time, but also supersedes time. The destiny that time is propelling us toward is entirely in Him.

The beginning and ending of everything that is exists in eternity, rather than on a timeline of history. And yet, our understanding of God and who we are in Him is playing out on a timeline that He created.

A Remnant within a Remnant

And it shall come to pass, that whosoever shall call on the name of the Lord *shall be delivered: for in mount Zion and in Jerusalem shall be deliverance, as the* Lord *hath said, and in* **the remnant whom the** Lord **shall call.**
Joel 2:32 (emphasis added)

Verily, verily, I say unto thee, Except a man be born again, he cannot see the kingdom of God. John 3:3

God has always had a remnant. At times is was one person or one family, as in the case of Noah and Abraham. At other times, it was a people group. The Israelites were a remnant of all the people on Earth, the Jews were a remnant of the twelve tribes of Israel, and the first Christians were a remnant of the Jews.

Today, there is a new remnant, which I believe Joel was referring to in Joel 2:32. It is interesting to me that he referred to Mount

Zion and to Jerusalem as being two different places in this prophetic word. Aren't they the same place geographically? Could it be that the distinction he made there was referring to Mount Zion as Israel and Jerusalem, or the New Jerusalem (see Revelation 3:12 and 21:2), as the true Church or the Body of Christ?

Many that go by the label "Christian" today are not born again (born from above) and they know the Lord only in name, if at all. But there is a remnant, the true Church, coming down from Heaven because they have first ascended up to Heaven, being seated with Christ in heavenly places (see Ephesians 2:6). From that vantage point, they have seen the Kingdom of God or Heaven coming *"in Earth as it is in Heaven,"* and as they descend into the systems of the world, they are imposing that Kingdom on the nations of the world.

But there is another remnant that is seeing the Kingdom more clearly than the remnant that is the New Jerusalem. This remnant has been marked by the rather intense and severe tests and trials they have endured, which has produced in them a trust in and an intimacy with God that only a few in the Body of Christ have experienced.

Those in the Church, the *ekklesia* (Greek for called out ones), have been called to be born again and seated in heavenly places in Christ Jesus. But those currently being brought to a place of deeper trust and intimacy are the chosen Bride of Christ.

At the present time, the entire Body of Christ is not the same as the Bride of Christ. Just as Eve was taken out of Adam in order to complete him, the Bride of Christ is currently being taken out of the Body of Christ in order to complete that Body. That's why some are finding it hard or impossible to continue "doing church" the way it has been done for so long now.

The New Jerusalem that Joel saw didn't look like the New Jerusalem that John saw. The New Jerusalem that Joel saw was separate from the remnant he spoke of. I believe Joel was prophesying the present time, when the Remnant Bride of Christ is being taken out of the Body of Christ, in order to complete that Body. The New Jerusalem that John saw was the completed Body of Christ, overcomers adorned as a bride for her husband (see Revelation 3:12 and 21:2).

Joel looked into the future and saw the Church we are seeing in the present time. John saw the Church of the future, which Paul spoke of in Ephesians 5:27 as *"a glorious church, not having spot, or wrinkle or any such thing," "holy and without blemish"*; or, in a word, *perfect*. This is the Church that the Remnant Bride of Christ is getting a glimpse of or a peep at.

From Glory to Glory

In the beginning was the Word, and the Word was with God, and the Word was God. And the Word was made flesh, and dwelt among us, (and we beheld his glory, the glory as of the only begotten of the Father,) full of grace and truth.

John 1:1 and 14

But we all, with open face beholding as in a glass the glory of the Lord, are changed into the same image from glory to glory, even as by the Spirit of the Lord.
2 Corinthians 3:18

Jesus was not only *in* the beginning; He *is* the Beginning, a glorious beginning full of grace and truth, which the original disciples beheld and which we, His present-day disciples, can also behold. But there is a remnant today that is not only beholding the glory of the Beginning that He is; we are getting a glimpse of or a peep into the even-more-glorious Ending that He is.

This is not about the so-called "end times" (which are not even mentioned in the Bible). The Bible does mention the *"last days,"* but that is only referring to the last days of the week. Peter said that a day is with the Lord as a thousand years and a thousand years as a day (see 2 Peter 3:8), so there is a parallel between the seven days of Creation and the seven millennia that the Bible focuses on. We are now in the last day (millennium), which is the third day (millennium) of the Church.

It is in this day (millennium), which is the Sabbath that all the Sabbaths of the Law and the Sabbath of Creation pointed the way to, that the Church will be perfected—becoming the Bride of Christ, the New Jerusalem that John saw, which only a remnant is able to comprehend at the present time. It is in this day that time, which is never ending, will be overwritten by eternity. And, I might add, this remnant within the remnant is getting a peep into that reality as well.

While we are not one hundred percent there yet, we have peeped into what it is to continually, perpetually and eternally go from glory to glory, which makes all the tests and trials we have endured worth the cost.

Making Peace

And let the peace of God rule in your hearts, to the which also ye are called … .
Colossians 3:15

This glory, that a remnant is tasting of and peeping into, is the end of the Beginning, which was complete in God before the foundation of the world, or since eternity. It is not an Ending subject to the confines of time, but rather an ending that is completion.

It is the destiny of this remnant to continue into this reality, finding the peace that passes all understanding (see Philippians 4:7), not only in their individual lives, but also reproducing that peace into the lives of others, eventually and ultimately encompassing the nations.

This is the ministry and word of reconciliation that is the Gospel of the Kingdom, which will produce the next and, perhaps, last Great Awakening and a new Reformation of the Church.

There has never been a day like this day. There has never been a time like this time. And, as I am compelled to say again and again, surely we were born *For Such a Time As This!*

Author Contact Information

- To schedule Lanny for your church meetings, conferences or other events
- To purchase additional copies of this book or Lanny's other books, *Kingdom Manna* and *Supernatural Encounters with God* (with reduced rates for quantities of ten or more)
- To purchase Lanny's music CDs, including his praise and worship CD entitled *For Such a Time as This*, recorded in Nashville and produced by Rick Sandidge of the Mark Five Company

Lanny Swaim
P.O. Box 217
Winnabow, NC 28479

lannyswaim@gmail.com

Lanny can also be contacted from his web site, where you can sign up for his emails, which include prophetic teaching, prophetic words, testimonies and revival reports.

www.lannyswaim.com

Kingdom Manna

God's Plan for Our
Changing World and
How You Can Make
a Difference

Prophetic Words, Teaching, & Testimony

Lanny Swaim

FOREWORD BY DR. ALVEDA KING

SUPERNATURAL
ENCOUNTERS
with *God*

A Spiritual Journey

LANNY SWAIM

Index of Scriptures Used

www.ingramcontent.com/pod-product-compliance
Lightning Source LLC
Chambersburg PA
CBHW031450070426
42452CB00037B/380